Celebrating Thanksgiving

BY JENNA LEE GLEISNER

The **Child's World®**
childsworld.com

Published by The Child's World®
1980 Lookout Drive • Mankato, MN 56003-1705
800-599-READ • www.childsworld.com

Photographs ©: Susan Chiang/iStockphoto, cover, 1;
Monkey Business Images/Shutterstock Images, 5; Titov
Dmitriy/Shutterstock Images, 6; Sergiy Bykhunenko/
Shutterstock Images, 9; Ryan McVay/Thinkstock, 11;
Monkey Business Images Ltd/Thinkstock,
12–13; Stepanek Photography/Shutterstock
Images, 15; Shutterstock Images, 16; Lev Radin/
Shutterstock Images, 19; Steve Debenport/
iStockphoto, 20

Design Element: Shutterstock Images

ISBN 9781503816626
LCCN 2016945660

Printed in the United States of America
PA02323

ABOUT THE AUTHOR
Jenna Lee Gleisner is an author
and editor from Minnesota. Her
favorite part about Thanksgiving is
spending time with family.

Contents

Fall Holiday

Today is Thanksgiving!
I play football with
my family.

Thanksgiving is in November. It is a fall **holiday**.

Fall is a time for **harvest**.

There is food to gather.

Time of Thanks

Thanksgiving is a time
to give thanks. We are
thankful for food.

We are thankful for family. We spend the day with family.

Thanksgiving Meal

My family eats a big meal. We eat turkey. We eat mashed potatoes.

Pumpkin pie is for dessert.
I put whipped cream
on top.

We watch a parade on TV. There are big balloons.

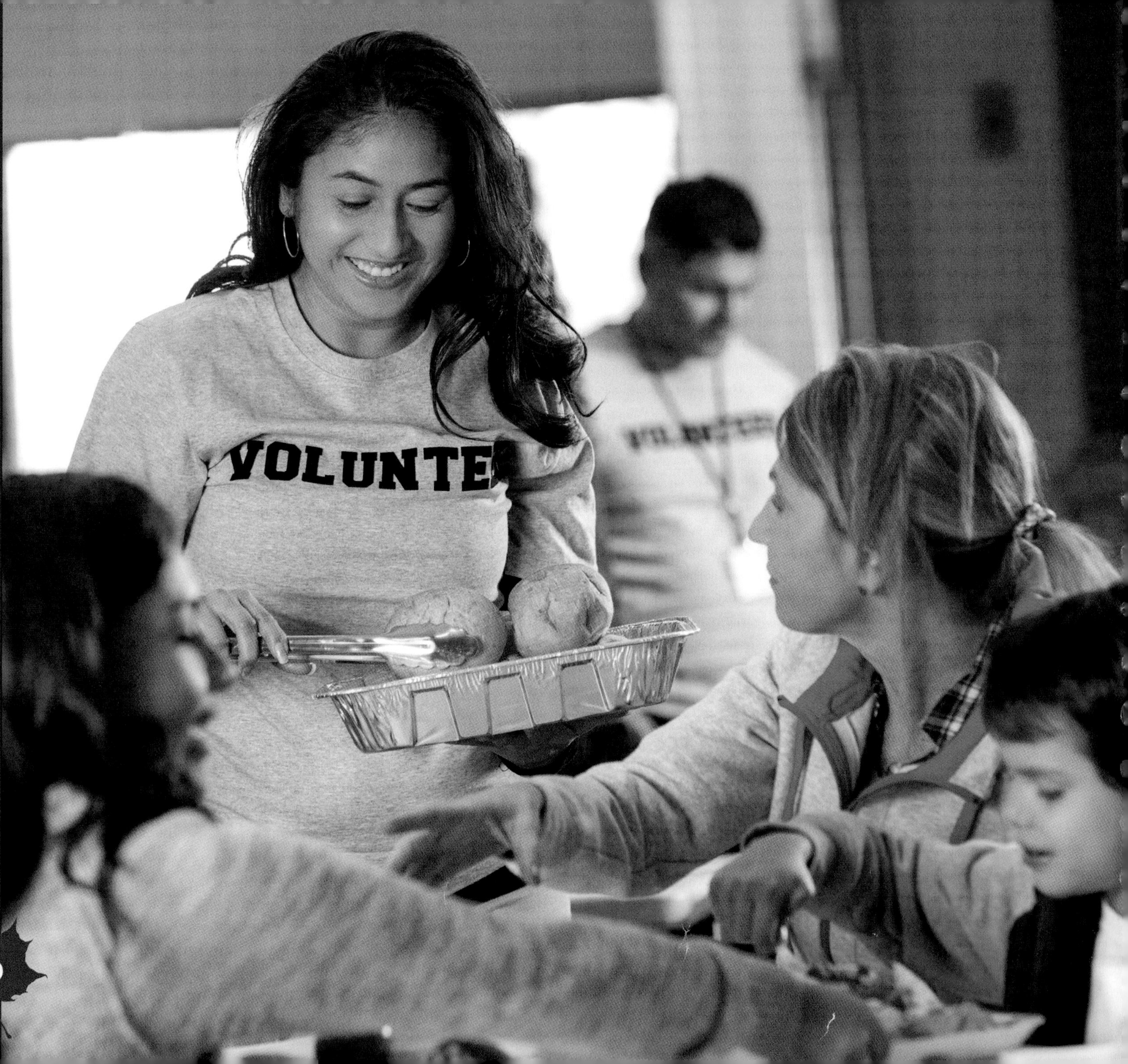
VOLUNTE

Then we **volunteer**. We feed others. How do you celebrate Thanksgiving?

Turkey Tube Craft

Make your own Thanksgiving turkey!

Supplies:

scissors

orange, yellow,
  and red construction
  paper

marker or crayon

glue

toilet paper tube

Instructions:

1. Have an adult help you cut feathers out of construction paper.

2. Write something you are thankful for on each feather.

3. Glue each feather to the paper tube.

4. Stand the paper tube upright.

5. Draw eyes and a beak.

Glossary

harvest — (HAHR-vist) To harvest means to gather crops from a field. We harvest food that is ready to eat in fall.

holiday — (HAH-li-day) A holiday is a day when people celebrate a special occasion. We celebrate the Thanksgiving holiday by giving thanks.

thankful — (THANGK-fuhl) To be thankful means to be grateful for what you have. On Thanksgiving, we are especially thankful for family and food.

volunteer — (vah-luhn-TEER) To volunteer is to do a job without getting paid. We volunteer our time to help feed people in need.

To Learn More

Books

Gulati, Annette. *Thanksgiving Crafts*. Mankato, MN: The Child's World, 2017.

Lawrence, Elizabeth. *Celebrate Thanksgiving*. New York, NY: Cavendish Square Publishing, 2016.

Web Sites

Visit our Web site for links about Thanksgiving: **childsworld.com/links**

Note to Parents, Teachers, and Librarians: We routinely verify our Web links to make sure they are safe and active sites. So encourage your readers to check them out!

Index